for Jenny

THIS IS A BOOK ABOUT GIRAFFES

Kestrel Books
Published by Penguin Books Ltd
Harmondsworth, Middlesex, England

ISBN 0 7226 5878 8

First Published 1983

Printed and bound in Singapore
for Sadie Fields Productions Ltd
866 United Nations Plaza, Suite 4030,
New York 10017 USA

THIS IS A BOOK ABOUT GIRAFFES

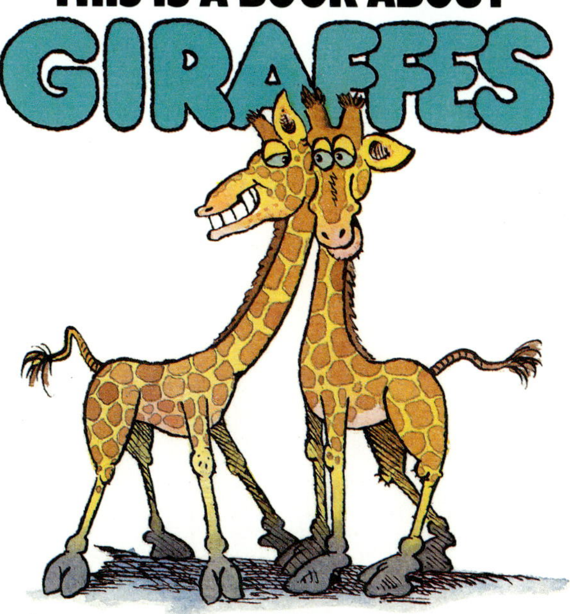

A FUN RHYME FOR CHILDREN

written by John Bush illustrated by Korky Paul

Kestrel Books

This is a book about giraffes.
Giraffes in tight knots

Giraffes in long socks
Giraffes, giraffes,
In flocks and flocks

Giraffes pulling faces

Giraffes running races

Giraffes in boots
With bright pink laces

Giraffes with big ears

Giraffes shedding tears

Giraffes sitting sipping
Iced ginger-beers

Giraffes stuck in marshes

Giraffes with moustaches

Giraffes on the beach
In their sunglasses

Giraffes dressed as clowns

Giraffes fallen down

Giraffes off to bed
In nightcap and gown

Giraffes doing hops

Giraffes in big pots

Giraffes with stripes
Instead of spots

Giraffes rather thinnish

Giraffes munching spinach

Giraffes from the start
Giraffes to the finish
As I said, if anyone asks
This is a book about

GIRAFFES